MARC SCOTT

A Beginner's Projects in Coding

illustrated by **MICK MARSTON**

BLOOMSBURY
CHILDREN'S BOOKS

NEW YORK LONDON OXFORD NEW DELHI SYDNEY

To James, the best code reviewer
a father could have

BLOOMSBURY CHILDREN'S BOOKS
Bloomsbury Publishing Inc., part of Bloomsbury Publishing Plc
1385 Broadway, New York, NY 10018

BLOOMSBURY, BLOOMSBURY CHILDREN'S BOOKS, and the Diana logo are trademarks of Bloomsbury Publishing Plc

First published in Great Britain in August 2016 as *A Beginner's Guide to Coding* by Bloomsbury Publishing Plc
First published in the United States of America in June 2017 as *A Beginner's Guide to Coding* by Bloomsbury Children's Books
Revised version published in March 2020

Bloomsbury books may be purchased for business or promotional use. For information on bulk purchases
please contact Macmillan Corporate and Premium Sales Deaprtment at specialmarkets@macmillan.com

Library of Congress Cataloging-in-Publication Data
available upon request
LCCN: 2019942857
ISBN:978-1-5476-0276-6

Printed in China by Leo Paper Products, Heshan, Guangdong
1 3 5 7 9 10 8 6 4 2

All papers used by Bloomsbury Publishing Inc. are natural, recyclable products made from wood grown in well-managed forests.
The manufacturing processes conform to the environmental regulations of the country of origin.

To find out more about our authors and books visit www.bloomsbury.com and sign up for our newsletters.

Scratch is developed by the Lifelong Kindergarten Group at the MIT Media Lab.
See http://scratch.mit.edu. The SCRATCH name and logos are trademarks owned by the Scratch Team.
For terms of use see: https://scratch.mit.edu/terms_of_use/

Contents

A guide to this book

What will I learn?

In the next few chapters you will learn how to use two different programming languages. The first language is called **Scratch** and the second is called **Python**. You will be able to complete exciting projects in each of the languages, with plenty of help to guide you as you learn to **program**.

It is very important to check with an adult before downloading anything onto your computer. This helps to keep you safe on the Internet, and will also keep your computer healthy!

How to use the tutorials

Learning to code is all about practicing and experimenting. Follow each of the tutorials carefully, and make sure you read the instructions as well as look at the picture guides.

Most importantly, once you have finished a tutorial, play around with your code. Try changing and adding extra bits, and don't worry if you break your code! All **programmers** make mistakes, and fixing those mistakes (called **debugging**) is the best way to learn.

Scratch Programming language created for children that uses blocks of code that can be connected together to make programs

Python Programming language based on typing text that is designed to be simple to learn and use

Program Design and write code

There's even a famous quote about coding and making mistakes by Mark Zuckerberg—the person who created Facebook:

Programmer Person who designs and writes code

Debugging Testing code to find and fix mistakes

"Move fast and break things. Unless you are breaking stuff, you are not moving fast enough."

What is coding?

What are computers?

Computers are all around us. There are probably lots of computers in your house; you might not realize how many! Do you or your family have a laptop? Of course, that is a computer. But what about a cell phone? Did you know that a cell phone is a computer too? There are even computers in your television, your microwave, and your car. Sometimes we use computers that are hundreds, or even thousands, of miles away. When you use the Internet, the computer (called a server) that stores the web page you are looking at could be in a completely different country from you.

Computers are machines that can work out the answers to very easy math problems. For instance, computers can add and subtract numbers, or they can tell if two numbers are the same. They can do math very quickly. If you tried to count to a million, it would probably take you over a week. A computer can count to a million in less than a second.

Being able to do math quickly is impressive, but the thing that makes computers really special is that they can follow instructions. These instructions are called **programs**. Computers can follow these instructions and do extremely clever things, like move monsters around the screen in a computer game or fly a real airplane to take you on a trip.

Without programs, a computer is completely useless. What actually makes computers so special is the programs that are written for them.

Programs
Collections of instructions that a computer follows to perform a task

What is coding?

When a programmer writes a computer program, they can't use any of the languages that people normally use to speak to each other.

You can't simply say to a computer, "Count to one thousand." Instead, you have to use a special language called a programming language. There are hundreds of different languages that you can write programs in. If we wanted a computer to count to one thousand in Scratch, a programming language you will soon be learning, we would write:

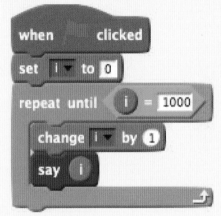

In Python, a language that you will learn later on in this book, we might instead write:

```
for i in range(1001):
    print(i)
```

In another language called JavaScript we would write:

```
for(i=0; i<1001; i++){
console.log(i)
};
```

The words and symbols used in programming languages are called **code**, so we often call writing computer programs **coding**.

Once you have finished writing a computer program, it needs to be translated into 1s and 0s. This is called **compiling** or **interpreting**, and allows the computer to read the instructions. It doesn't matter which programming language you use; the computer translates it into 1s and 0s.

Compiling
Converting a program into a language that a computer can run

Interpreting
When a program is run by a computer, one line at a time

Code
Instructions written in a programming language that a computer can follow

Coding
Writing code for a computer

What is syntax?

Syntax is the rules of a language. Look at these two sentences:

"I am an awesome coder."

"coder am an I awesome."

The first sentence makes sense because it follows the syntax (or rules) of the English language. The second sentence doesn't follow the rules and doesn't make sense. You could probably work out what the sentence means, even though the words are in the wrong order, because you are an intelligent person. But computers aren't intelligent in the same way as you! They can't work out what you mean when you write code that isn't correct.

If you don't follow the rules of the programming language, the computer will not try to compile or interpret the instructions; instead, it will just tell you that you've made a mistake. This is called a **syntax error**.

Syntax
The rules of a programming language

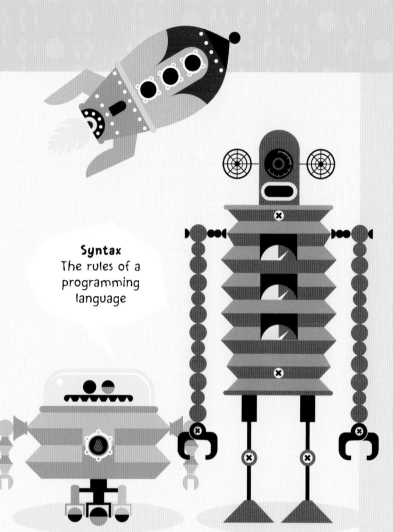

Syntax error
Mistake in a computer program caused by not following the rules of the programming language

Why is coding important?

There are computers everywhere, and they are doing many important jobs every day. We use computers to learn, to work, to play, to talk, to travel . . . and every time we use a computer, it works by running code that was written by a programmer.

Getting ready to SCRATCH

Scratch is a programming language that was designed to teach coding. You'll get the hang of it in no time, and then you can use it to create games, interactive stories, and animations.

Before you start using Scratch, you're going to need to create an account. If you are under 13 years old, you will need to talk to an adult and use their email address.

Setting up a Scratch account

1. Open up a web browser on your computer.
2. You need to go to **www.scratch.mit.edu**
3. You should see a **Join Scratch** button that you can click on.
4. Next you will need to choose a username and a password. Make sure you do not use your real name. Click **Next** when you are done.

Names on the Internet

The Internet is a great place to meet and talk to new people, but you don't always know who you are talking to and whether you can trust them. You should always pick usernames that are different from your real name. Choose a favorite game, a cartoon character, or even a pet's name.

Passwords

Passwords make sure nobody can use your account and pretend to be you. You should choose a password that nobody would be able to guess. It is a good idea to use a **passphrase** like:

ILoveEatingHats

or

MyFishNeverSleeps

Passphrase Group of words that is easy to remember but hard for someone else to guess

Join Scratch

Your responses to these questions will be kept private.
Why do we ask for this info ❓

Birth Month and Year	January ⬍	2008 ⬍
Gender	⦿ Male ◯ Female ◯	
Country	United Kingdom ⬍	

5. Now you need to add in your age, gender, and location before clicking on Next .

Join Scratch   X

Enter your parent's or guardian's email address and we will send them an email to confirm this account.

| Parent's or guardian's email address | my-parent@email.com |
| Confirm email address | my-parent@email.com |

1 — 2 — 3 — 4 — ✉   Next

6. For the next part you will need a helpful adult. Ask them to fill in their email address in the spaces provided. They can check their email later to confirm their address.

Join Scratch   X

Welcome to Scratch, **awesome-coder-321**!

You're now logged in! You can start exploring and creating projects.

If you want to share and comment, simply click the link in the email we sent you at ▬▬▬▬▬▬▬▬

Wrong email? Change your email address in Account Settings.

Having problems? Please give us feedback

1 — 2 — 3 — 4 — ✉   OK Lets Go!

7. If you see a screen like this one, then it means you have been registered with the Scratch website, and you're ready to start coding!

8. Click on the OK Lets Go! button, to begin exploring Scratch.

9

Getting around

To understand the projects in this book, you are going to need to know a little bit about the Scratch **Graphical User Interface** (GUI).

1. On the main page, click on **Create**.

2. You should see a screen like the one pictured here.

The **Toolbar** is where you can choose options like saving your project or creating a new one.

Toolbar

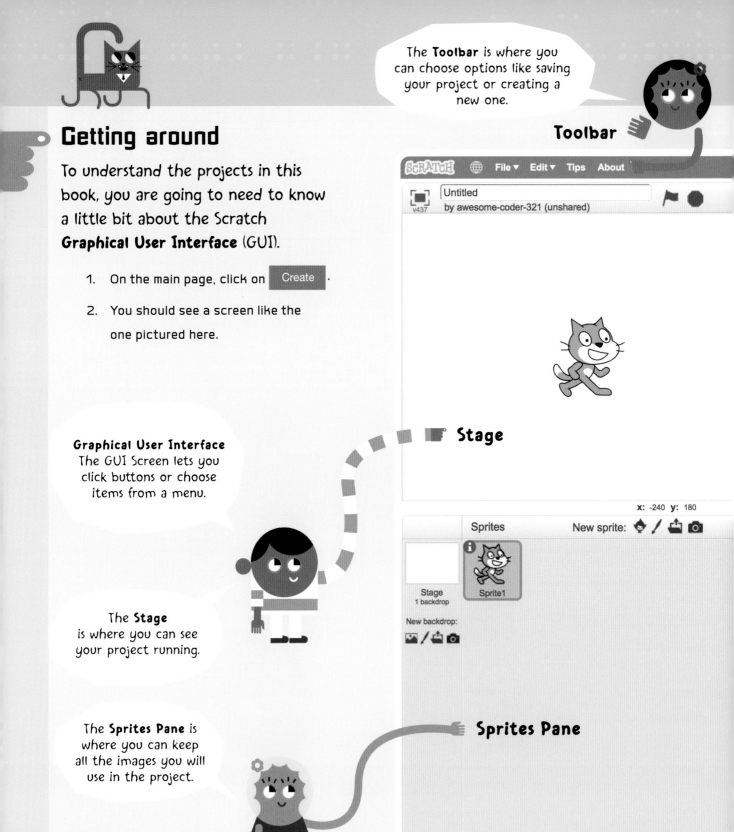

Stage

Graphical User Interface
The GUI Screen lets you click buttons or choose items from a menu.

The **Stage** is where you can see your project running.

Sprites Pane

The **Sprites Pane** is where you can keep all the images you will use in the project.

The **Script Area** is where you will place all your code for the project.

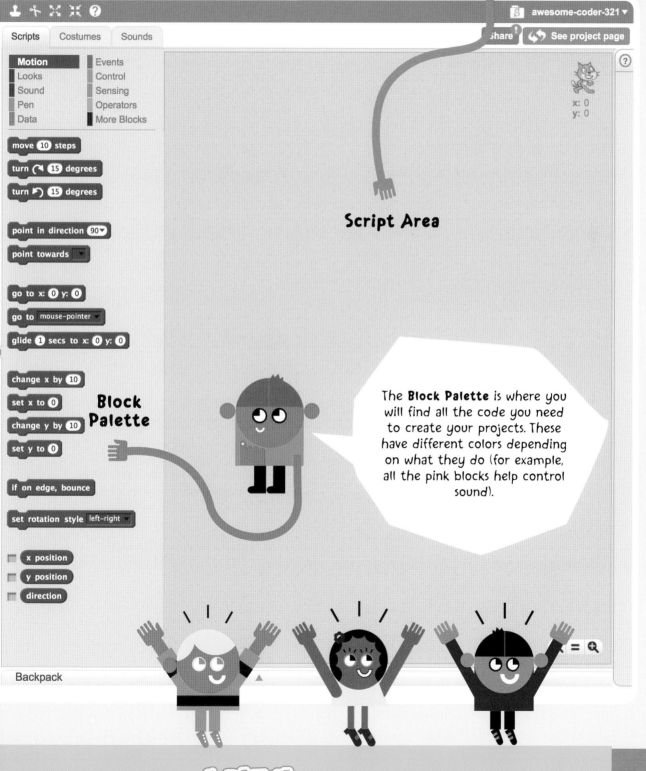

Script Area

The **Block Palette** is where you will find all the code you need to create your projects. These have different colors depending on what they do (for example, all the pink blocks help control sound).

Block Palette

Now that you know a little bit about SCRATCH let's start on the next chapter and code your first project!

¡Hola mundo!

When coders are learning a new language, often the first program they write is called the "Hello World!" program. This teaches the coder how to show text on the screen, like words or numbers. In this chapter, you are going to learn how to show some text on the screen, but you will also learn how to use Scratch extensions to get your computer to speak in different languages.

1. Let's begin by making a new custom block. Custom blocks are really useful. They help you keep your code tidy and make it easy to reuse code that you have written lots of times. In the 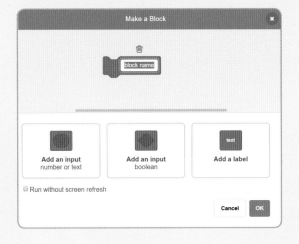 Code menu, click on My Blocks and then click on Make a Block .

   You should see a dialogue box like this one:

Make a Block
block name
Add an input — number or text / Add an input — boolean / text Add a label
Run without screen refresh
Cancel OK

2. Currently the block is called "block name," but you can change this so that it is called "say it."

3. You can add code to the bottom of the  define say it block.

   For now, you can keep it very simple. In the Looks menu, find the say Hello! block and drag it onto your Script Area. It should connect with the define say it block.

   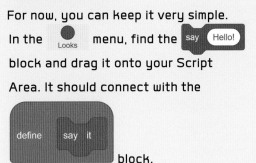

4. You can change the text in the 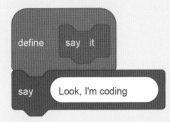 block to anything you like.

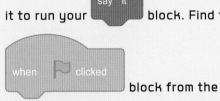

5. The code you have written is for the cat sprite called "Sprite1." To get the cat to actually say the words, you'll need to tell it to run your 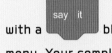 block. Find the

when ⚑ clicked block from the ◯ Events menu. Add this to your Script Area along with a say it block from the ● My Blocks menu. Your complete script should look like this

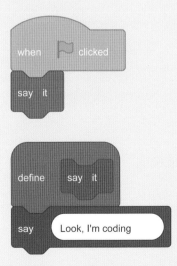

6. Now, near the top of the screen, click on the green flag to run your script. Does the cat say the words you have told it to? Well done—you've written your first Scratch program!

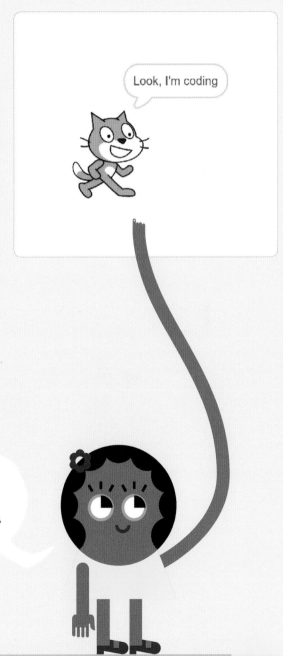

Look, I'm coding

Sprites
Images used in
computer games

Let's change your program to make it a little more useful. You can make your sprite say whatever the person who is using the program types in.

1. To begin, you can edit your

    block by right-clicking on it and then clicking on "Edit."

2. You should see a dialogue box like this one:

   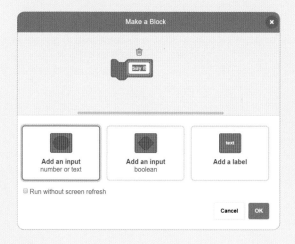

   Now click on "Add an input—number or text."

3. Now change the  block so that it says "words" instead. Then drag the "words" block into the "say" block.

4. On your Script Area, your custom block should now look like this:

   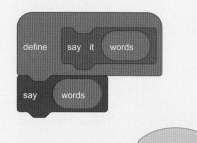

5. Now, underneath the 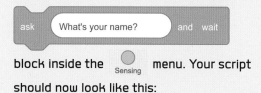 block, you can ask the user what they want the sprite to say. You can find the ask block inside the Sensing menu. Your script should now look like this:

Script
Small section of code, which can be as short as a few lines or as long as hundreds of lines. In Scratch, a script is a collection of blocks that you have joined together.

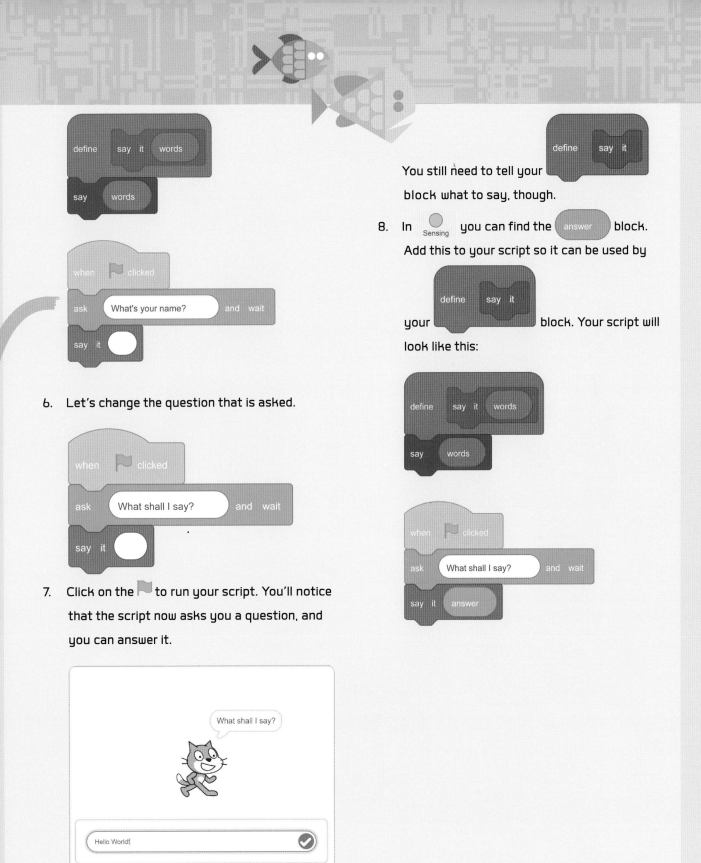

You still need to tell your block what to say, though.

8. In Sensing you can find the answer block. Add this to your script so it can be used by your define say it block. Your script will look like this:

6. Let's change the question that is asked.

7. Click on the 🏳 to run your script. You'll notice that the script now asks you a question, and you can answer it.

Excellent. You've made a program using **input** and **output**. The input is the text you type in. The output is the text that the sprite says. And with Scratch, you can have other types of output besides typed words. We can make the sprite actually talk!

1. First you need to click on the ⬱ button to add an extension. In the menu that opens, select the "Text to Speech" extension.

Text to Speech
Make your projects talk.

2. Now click on the new ◀💬 Text to Speech menu in your 🔲 Code menu and drag the speak hello block so that it sits underneath your define say it block. You can then drag in a words block so that your script looks like this:

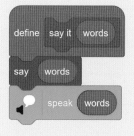

3. Now click on the ⚑ and type something. The sprite should say the words out loud!

Now let's change the script so your sprite can talk in different languages.

1. You're going to ask the user of your program what language they want to translate the words into. This means asking another question. You can only save one answer at a time, though, so you're going to use a variable to store the words and the language.

   Click on 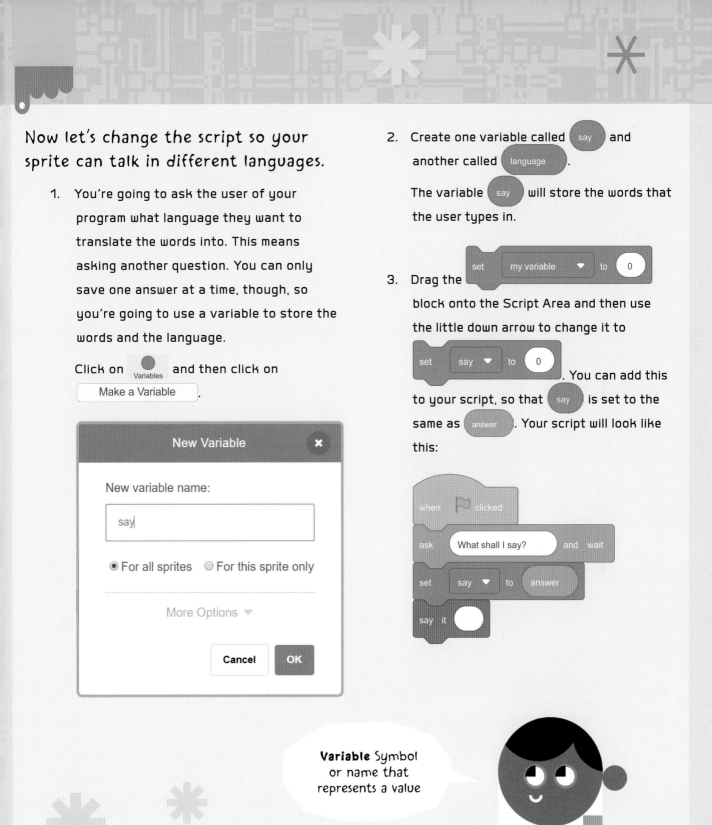 **Variables** and then click on **Make a Variable**.

   ### New Variable   ✖

   New variable name:

   | say| |

   ⦿ For all sprites   ◯ For this sprite only

   More Options ▾

   Cancel   **OK**

2. Create one variable called `say` and another called `language`.

   The variable `say` will store the words that the user types in.

   set my variable ▼ to 0

3. Drag the block onto the Script Area and then use the little down arrow to change it to

   set say ▼ to 0 . You can add this to your script, so that `say` is set to the same as `answer`. Your script will look like this:

   when 🏳 clicked

   ask What shall I say? and wait

   set say ▼ to answer

   say it ○

Variable Symbol or name that represents a value

4. Next you can drag a `say` block into your

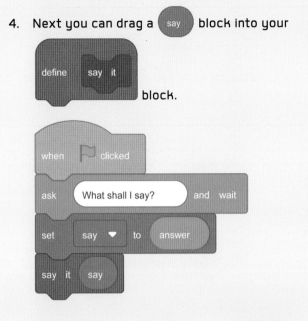

block.

5. Next you can do the same for the `language` variable. Ask the user what language they want to use and save their answer in your `language` variable.

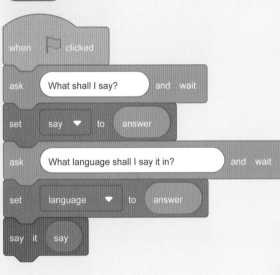

6. To finish off, you will need to edit your

define `say it`

block to make it translate the words.

Right-click on the block, select "Edit" and then "Add an input—number or text." Call this input "language." Your custom block will change to look like this:

7. Now you need to add the "Translate" extension, just like you added the "Text to Speech" extension before.

Translate

Translate text into many languages.

8. From the ![Translate icon] Translate menu, select the

translate (hello) to (Macedonian ▼)

block and drag it to your Script Area. It can then be placed into the

define say it

block to replace the

words blocks that were there.

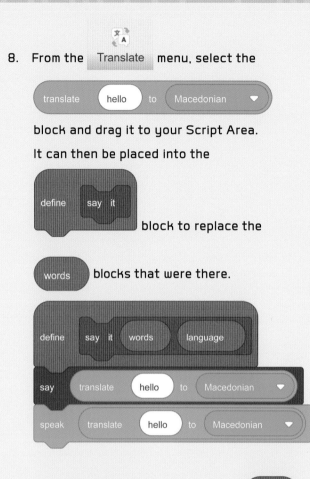

9. To finish off this program, drag the words and language blocks down into the translate blocks.

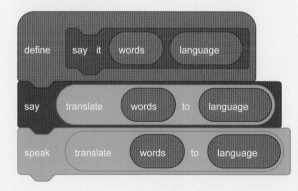

10. Then alter the starting script so that the (say) and (language) variables are used in the [say it ◯ ◯] block:

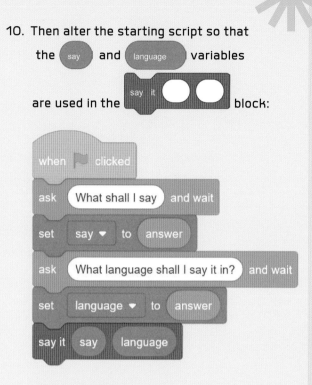

Click on the ⚑ to run your program. You should be asked what you want to say and the language you want to say it in. Your Scratch program will do the rest, reading out and saying your words in another language.

Create a music video

In this project, you're going to create your very own music video, complete with a dancer, flashing lights, and a disco ball.

Set the stage

1. You can begin by creating a set for your music video. To do this, you need to choose a new backdrop for your stage. Hover your mouse pointer over the icon. Then click on "Choose a Backdrop."

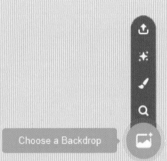

Here, the "Concert" backdrop has been chosen and is displayed on the stage.

2. You don't need the white background anymore. Make sure you've selected the backdrop you are using by clicking on the image on the right side of the screen.

Then select the "Backdrops" tab, right-click on the blank backdrop, and select "Delete."

3. Now that you have a backdrop, you can add some code to it to make it more exciting. Click on the "Code" tab.

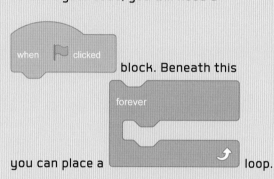

To start your code, you will need a

block. Beneath this

you can place a loop.
Forever loops are used to contain code that you want to repeat until your program ends.

4. Inside the 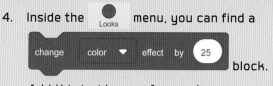 menu, you can find a

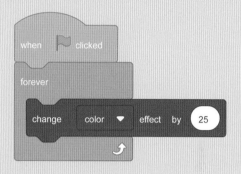 block.

Add this inside your forever loop.

Now click on the 🚩, and your backdrop should flash in different colors.

5. You can try out different effect sizes. Try changing the value from 25 to something else, and see what happens.

6. If you find that the flashing is too fast, you can add a block and then choose a new number. This will slow down your forever loop.

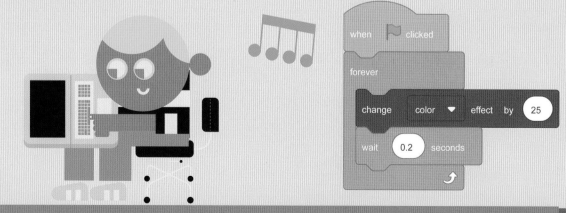

Get dancing

You need to find a dancer for your stage.

1. First delete the cat sprite by clicking on the x in the blue circle in the corner of the icon, or by right-clicking on it and selecting "Delete."

2. Click on the 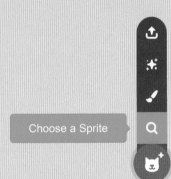 icon, and select the "Choose a Sprite" option.

3. You'll want one of the dancing sprites for this project. Search using the word "Dance," and then choose one of the sprites. Hovering your mouse over them will show you their moves.

4. Click on the "Costumes" tab for your sprite to see all the different costume options. Quickly changing the sprite's costumes (positions) will make it look like it is dancing.

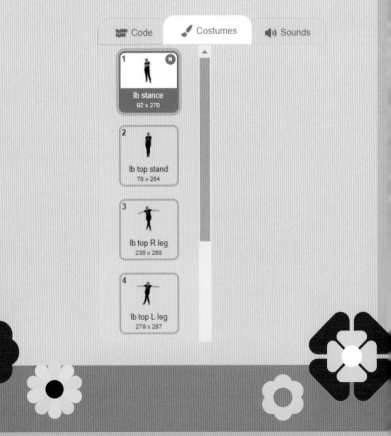

5. Click back on the "Code" tab. Start with a

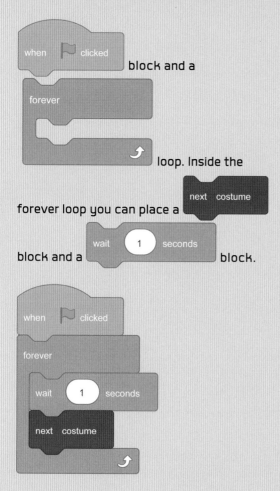

when [flag] clicked block and a

forever loop. Inside the

forever loop you can place a next costume

block and a wait 1 seconds block.

when [flag] clicked
forever
  wait 1 seconds
  next costume

6. Click on the [flag] again and watch your sprite dance as your backdrop flashes. Change the wait time until you like the animation.

7. You can click and drag your sprite around the stage until you find the right position for it to stand. You can also change the size of the sprite.

| Sprite | LB Dance | x | -70 | y | -8 |
| Size | 60 | Direction | 90 |

Add some tunes

Next you're going to want some music to go with your video. There are lots of music tracks in Scratch that you can use, or you can upload your own.

1. Click on the "Sounds" tab for your sprite.

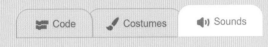

2. You'll probably see a sound already there. Click on the ▶ icon to hear the music.

3. If you want to choose some different music, click on the 🔊 icon and select "Choose a Sound."

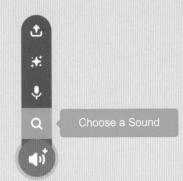

4. Pick a sound from the "Loops" menu. Hovering over a sound will play it for you.

You might have your own mp3 music file you want to use, or maybe you've found one on the Internet, from a website like http://freemusicarchive.org.

1. Click on the "Sounds" tab and then delete the sound that is there by clicking on the blue x, or right-clicking and selecting "Delete."

2. Click on the  icon and select "Upload Sound."

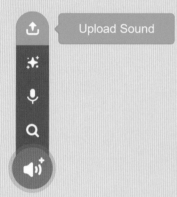

3. Select your saved sound from your files, and your new sound should appear.

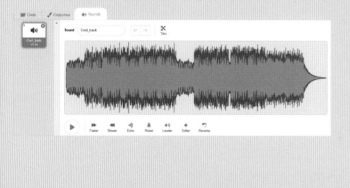

Looping your track

Now you want to play your sound forever, until you stop your program.

1. Go back to the "Code" tab to add some more code to your sprite.

You will need another

block and a loop.

2. This time, inside the forever loop, add the

play sound **Cool_track** ▼ until done

block.

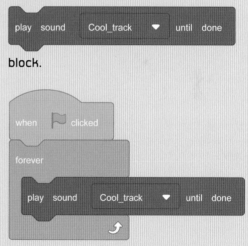

3. Now that you have your music playing, you can change your wait times so that the backdrop flashes and the player dances in time to the music.

Add some props

Now you can add some props to your music video to make it more exciting.

1. Use an image search to find a picture of a disco ball online, and download it to your computer.

2. Click on the  icon, and choose "Upload."

3. Select the image of the disco ball and upload it to Scratch.

4. Resize and position your disco ball on the stage.

5. To finish off this section, you can make the disco ball move! See if you can find the following blocks and add them to the disco ball's scripts to make it spin.

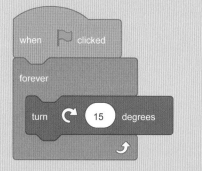

6. You could try to add some more props to the stage and animate them. How about a speaker that booms in time to the music, or maybe a laser that moves around the stage? Can you add another dancer to the scene? Maybe you could make the backdrop change as the music changes.

Hungry, hungry hare

In this project, you're going to take your first steps in creating your very own computer game. The player will take control of a hungry hare that must move around the screen and collect strawberries to eat before the time runs out.

1. Create a new Scratch project, and then delete the cat sprite.

2. Create a new sprite by clicking on 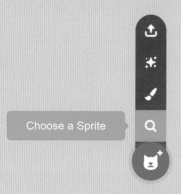 and then selecting "Choose a Sprite."

   Choose a Sprite

3. Choose the "Hare" sprite from the "Animals" menu.

4. Click on the "Costumes" tab to look at the hare's three costumes (positions).

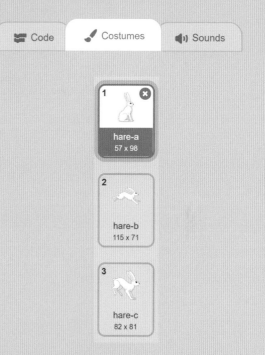

The hare has three costumes, and they are all facing right. You are going to need all the costumes, and you'll need some that face left too. In the "Costumes" tab, you can change the names of the costumes. Change the names of all three costumes, so that "hare-a" becomes "hare-a-right," "hare-b" becomes "hare-b-right," and "hare-c" becomes "hare-c-right."

5. Make a copy of the first costume by right-clicking it and selecting "Duplicate" from the menu. Change the name of the new costume to "hare-a-left."

> duplicate
> delete

hare-a-right
57 x 98

hare-a-right
57 x 98

2
hare-a-left
57 x 98

6. Now you can edit the costume to make the hare face to the left. In the "Costumes" tab, click on the 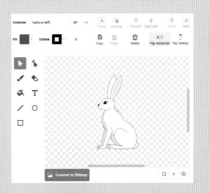 button and the hare will flip to face the left.

Do the same for the other two costumes, so that you have six in total—three facing right and three facing left.

1
hare-a-right
57 x 98

2
hare-a-left
56 x 98

3
hare-b-right
115 x 71

4
hare-b-left
114 x 70

5
hare-c-right
82 x 81

6
hare-c-left
81 x 81

Now that you have the costumes, it's time to make your hare move.

7. Click on the "Code" tab, and then from the  menu, select [Make a Variable]. Call your new variable "direction."

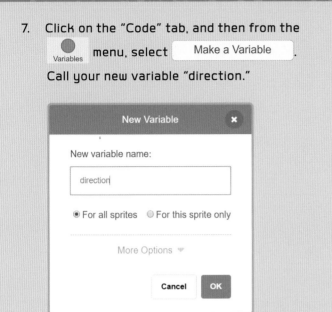

8. At the start of the game, the hare should face right. Add this script to your hare to set the variable at the start of the game.

9. Add a [forever] loop so that you can check the direction of the hare at all times during the game.

10. Inside the 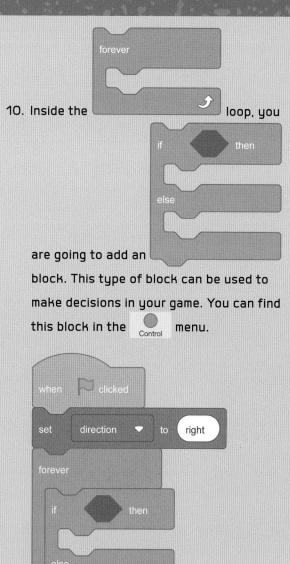 forever loop, you are going to add an

block. This type of block can be used to make decisions in your game. You can find this block in the Control menu.

11. Click on the Operators menu. You will find a diamond-shaped block with an equal sign inside it, like this: $\bigcirc = 50$. Drag this into the graphic block.

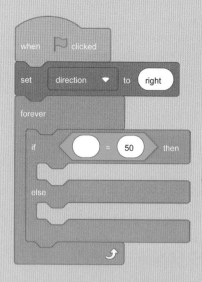

This operator can be used to check if the direction variable is equal to left or right.

12. In the menu, find the `direction` variable and add it to the script, checking to see if the variable's value is left or right.

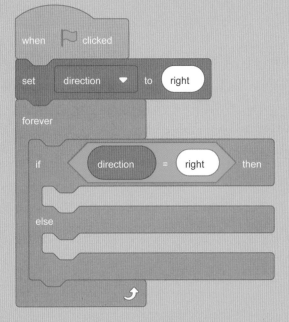

If the hare is facing right, then the costume you use should be "hare-a-right." If it's not, then the costume you need is "hare-a-left."

Now you can make some custom blocks to actually move the hare.

13. Use the  menu to create two new blocks. One should be called "right" and the other called "left."

These blocks will be used to make the hare move to the right and left sides of the screen. You can start with the

block.

14. The first thing the block should do is make sure the `direction` variable is set to "right" and then change the costume to "hare-b-right."

15. Now the position of the hare sprite needs to change. On computers, the horizontal position of a sprite is often called its x position. If x is increased, a sprite would move right. If x is decreased, then the sprite would move left.

Look in the 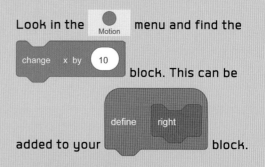 menu and find the

block. This can be

added to your block.

16. Change the value to 5.

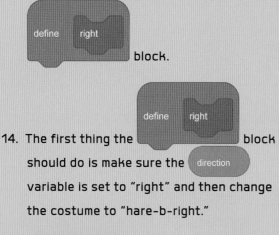

You can test whether this works by clicking

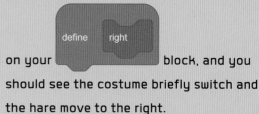 on your block, and you should see the costume briefly switch and the hare move to the right.

17. Now you can make the hare look like it is running. Add blocks to your script until it looks like the one below. You should know where to find all the blocks by now.

Again, you can test this out by clicking on the  block a few times.

18. Now do the same for the block. This time, though, you will need to change x by -5 and use the left-facing costumes:

```
define    left

set    direction ▼ to    left

switch  costume  to    hare-b-left ▼

change  x by   -5

wait    0.05   seconds

switch  costume  to    hare-c-left ▼

change  x by   -5

wait    0.05   seconds
```

19. To finish off the code for your hare, you need to use the blocks you have made to recognize when a specific key is pressed on the keyboard.

In your starting script, in the forever loop, your program needs to constantly check if a key has been pressed. Add in two

```
if        then
```

blocks, like this.

20. Look in the 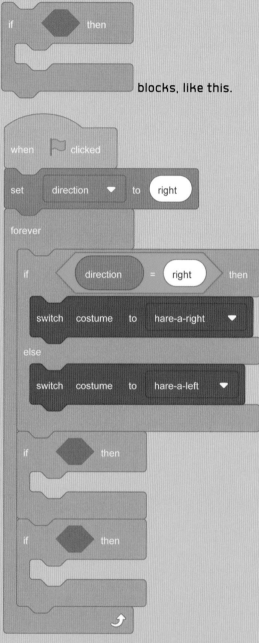 Sensing menu and find the

```
key  space  ▼  pressed
```

block. These blocks detect key presses. Add them into

```
if        then
```

the block, but change the key presses to the "left" and "right" arrow keys.

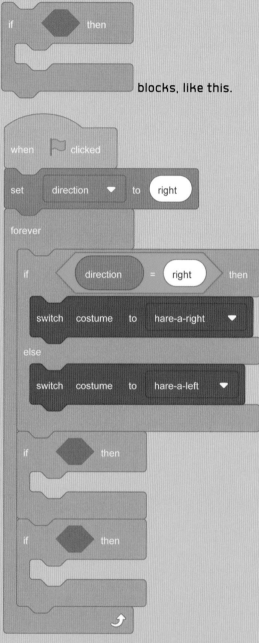

```
when 🏳 clicked

set   direction  ▼  to  right

forever
    if   direction  =  right  then
        switch  costume  to  hare-a-right  ▼
    else
        switch  costume  to  hare-a-left  ▼

    if        then

    if        then
```

when 🚩 clicked

set [direction ▼] to (right)

forever

  if < (direction) = (right) > then

    switch costume to [hare-a-right ▼]

  else

    switch costume to [hare-a-left ▼]

  if < key [left arrow ▼] pressed? > then

  if < key [right arrow ▼] pressed? > then

---

21. Last, you can place your custom blocks

if < ⬡ > then

inside the [ ] blocks.

when 🚩 clicked

set [direction ▼] to (right)

forever

  if < (direction) = (right) > then

    switch costume to [hare-a-right ▼]

  else

    switch costume to [hare-a-left ▼]

  if < key [left arrow ▼] pressed? > then

    left

  if < key [right arrow ▼] pressed? > then

    right

Test out your script by clicking on the 🚩 and then using the arrow keys on your keyboard to move your hare left and right.

Now that you have a sprite you can move around the screen, let's add a bit of scenery to the game.

22. Choose a backdrop for your game by clicking on 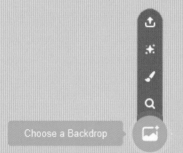 in the bottom righthand corner of the screen and then choosing a backdrop.

The backdrop you choose is up to you, but here is the one we used in our version of the game.

You might want to move your hare around so that it appears to be sitting on the ground.

Now, let's give the hare some food to eat.

23. Add a new sprite to your game by clicking on . Then select an icon from the  menu. In this version of the

project, we will use a 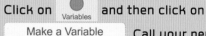 .

24. As the hare eats strawberries, the player's score will increase. You can use a variable to store the value of the player's score. Click on ⬤ Variables and then click on Make a Variable . Call your new variable "score."

New Variable ✕

New variable name:

score

● For all sprites   ○ For this sprite only

More Options ▼

Cancel   OK

At the start of the game, the player's score should be zero.

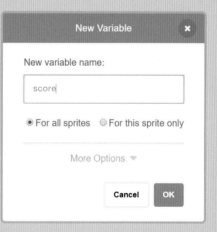

25. Now position the strawberry on the screen and set its size using another code block.

```
when [flag] clicked
set score to 0
set size to 40 %
```

26. To make lots of food for the hare to eat, you're going to generate **clones** of the strawberry. Clones are exact copies of an item.

27. Hide the strawberry and then use a

```
forever
```

loop to make a new clone of the strawberry every second.

```
when [flag] clicked
set score to 0
set size to 40 %
forever
    create clone of myself
    wait 1 seconds
```

28. Next you will need to make sure that the clones can be seen and then move them to a random position.

```
when I start as a clone
show
go to x: pick random 230 to -230 y: -150
```

Click on the [flag] to test that your program is working. You should see strawberries appearing across the ground on the screen.

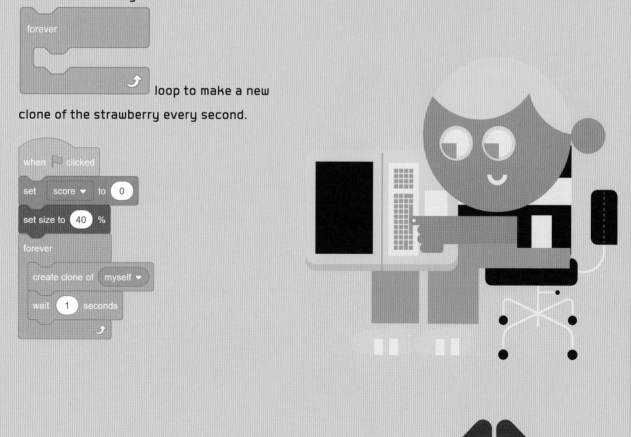

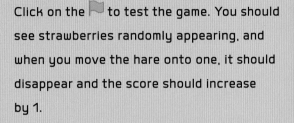

29. Each time the hare touches a strawberry, the clone should be deleted and the player's score should increase.

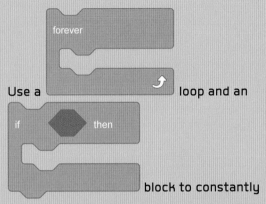

Use a loop and an

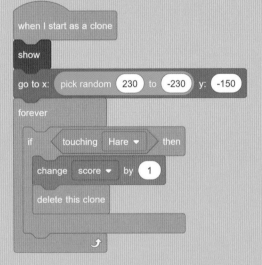 block to constantly detect if the hare is touching a strawberry clone.

```
when I start as a clone
show
go to x: pick random 230 to -230 y: -150
forever
    if     touching Hare ▾    then
        change score ▾ by 1
        delete this clone
```

Click on the ⚑ to test the game. You should see strawberries randomly appearing, and when you move the hare onto one, it should disappear and the score should increase by 1.

30. To finish off, the game needs a time limit, so that the player can't just keep getting points forever.

Start a new script using a

 block. Then "reset" the timer that is built into Scratch.

```
when 🏳 clicked
reset timer
```

```
forever
⟲
```

Use a loop and an

```
if ⬡ then
```

block to detect if the timer has gone beyond 10 seconds. If it has, the game can end by stopping all the scripts.

```
when 🏳 clicked
reset timer
forever
  if  timer > 10  then
    stop  all ▼
  ⟲
```

31. Click on the 🏳 to test your game and see how many strawberries you can collect in 10 seconds.

Are you ready for Python?

Python

Python is a programming language, just like Scratch, but instead of moving and joining blocks, you write your code using text.

Python was created by a man called Guido van Rossum. It is a little harder to use than Scratch, but it is a very powerful language. Well-known companies like Google and Apple use Python to write some of their **software**.

When you write code in Python it looks like this:

```
def sayHello():
    print("Hello")
sayHello()
```

You are going to learn how to use the version of Python which is called Python 3. Start off by asking an adult to help you install Python 3 on your computer by visiting **https://www.python.org/downloads**

There you should find a link to download and install Python 3.

Once you have installed Python you should find a new program called IDLE on your computer. You can write Python code with lots of different programs, but as a beginner, it is easiest to use IDLE.

Software
Programs or collections of programs that run on your computer. Your web browser is a type of software, as is IDLE, which you'll be using in this chapter.

A quick note on deleting
Once you have pressed "enter," you can't delete the commands you have written.

Don't worry if you make a mistake—you can just type your code again correctly.

IDLE

1. Find IDLE and open it. Now you can start to learn how to code with Python! Depending on your computer, IDLE might look slightly different from the pictures in this book. But don't worry, this will not affect your code. What you are now looking at is the Python **shell**:

```
Python 3.4.3 (default, Jun 10 2015, 19:56:14)
[GCC 4.2.1 Compatible Apple LLVM 6.1.0 (clang-602.0.53)] on darwin
Type "copyright", "credits" or "license()" for more information.
>>> |
```

> **Shell** Program that follows written instructions

The shell is a little like the Stage in Scratch, but it will only display text. It doesn't look as fun as Scratch, but it can do some cool things, as you'll soon find out! The shell is a place where you can write code that will be run right away. It's a great place to test small lines of code to see what they do.

2. Unlike the Stage in Scratch, in Python we can type code straight into the shell. Try typing the following commands and see what happens. Press "enter" on your keyboard after each one.

```
10+10
10-5
10*5
10/5
print("Hello")

print("Hello" * 100)
```

Syntax

Do you remember from the first chapter how important syntax is? Let's test that out.

1. Try typing the following command in the shell:

```
print("Hello)
```

2. You should get an error message telling you "SyntaxError: EOL while scanning string literal." This just means you forgot to place a " after the word "Hello."

3. Try typing the command again, with the " after the word.

Be prepared to make lots of mistakes and get lots of warnings like this. Remember, programmers learn by making mistakes and then trying to figure out what they did wrong. Even the best programmers in the world make silly mistakes like forgetting to put a " in their code.

Turtles all the way

Some turtley awesome commands

1. Open IDLE. We're going to play around with a part of Python called "turtle." This is a module used for drawing with Python.

> **Module**
> Code that has been written by other people that you can use in your own programs. Programmers don't like rewriting code that already exists, so they use modules to help speed things up.

2. In the shell, type the following command and press "enter." Don't worry if nothing happens.

   ```
   from turtle import *
   ```

3. Remember that syntax is important. Make sure you type everything as shown. The "*" character is normally found by using "shift" and "8."

4. We're going to give our turtle a shape. Type this into the shell.

   ```
   shape("turtle")
   ```

5. A new screen will appear, with a picture of a turtle in the middle. It is best to arrange your screens side by side, like this:

```
                   Python 3.4.3 Shell
Python 3.4.3 (default, Jul  3 2015, 01:28:31)
[GCC 4.2.1 Compatible Apple LLVM 6.1.0 (clang-6
02.0.53)] on darwin
Type "copyright", "credits" or "license()" for
more information.

>>> from turtle import *
>>> shape("turtle")
>>>
```

6. Now let's move our turtle around. Type this into the shell:

```
fd(100)
rt(90)
fd(100)
```

You might have realized that "fd" means "forward" and "rt" means "right." We can also use "bk" for "backward" and "lt" for "left." If we type "lt (90)" it means turning our turtle by 90 degrees:

```
bk(100)
lt(90)
```

7. Now try moving the turtle around the screen. Change the numbers in the brackets to turn and move it by different values.

8. Try to draw some different shapes with the turtle. If you lose it you can always bring it home by typing:

```
home()
```

Controlling the turtle's pen

1. Let's bring our turtle home and then clear the screen of our drawings so far.

```
home()
clear()
```

You can do this anytime you want to start a fresh drawing.

2. We can also control the color and width of the pen that our turtle uses to draw. Try this:

```
fd(50)
color("red")
fd(50)
color("green")
width(10)
fd(50)
```

3. We can lift the pen up and put it down again, if we want to stop and start drawing.

```
home()
clear()
fd(100)
pu()
fd(100)
pd()
fd(100)
```

4. If you make a mistake, you can always undo the last command:

```
undo()
```

5. Let's try one final command before you start the challenges. This is how you tell the turtle to draw a circle:

```
circle(100)
```

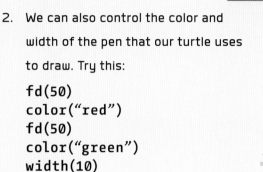

Can you take a challenge?

- Can you draw a square with the turtle?

- How about a triangle?

- Can you draw a circle with a cross through it?

Loopy shapes

Saving your turtle

We have been writing all our commands in the shell up until now. This is easy to do, but it means that we lose all the fun pictures we have made when we close IDLE.

We can save our code if we stop writing in the shell and use files instead.

1. In IDLE click on "File" and then "New File."

File	Edit	Shell	Debug
New File			⌘N
Open…			⌘O
Open Module…			
Recent Files			▶
Class Browser			⌘B
Path Browser			
Close			⌘W
Save			⌘S
Save As…			⇧⌘S
Save Copy As…			⌥⌘S
Print Window			⌘P

2. Another window should open. This is where you can write all your code. We can start in the same way we did before:

```
from turtle import *
shape("turtle")
```

3. Nothing happens when you press "enter" on your keyboard this time. This is because we aren't in the shell. We need to choose "Save" and "Run" to see the file working. You can do this from the menu bar like this:

File	Edit	Shell	Debug
New File			⌘N
Open…			⌘O
Open Module…			
Recent Files			▶
Class Browser			⌘B
Path Browser			
Close			⌘W
Save			**⌘S**
Save As…			⇧⌘S
Save Copy As…			⌥⌘S
Print Window			⌘P

4. The first time you save, you will need to name the file. Call it "poly.py." Then you can click "Run."

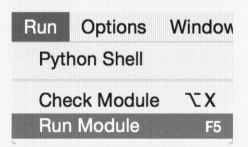

Run	Options	Window
Python Shell		
Check Module		⌥X
Run Module		**F5**

45

A note on shortcuts

It's easier to use shortcut keys than always using the menus in files.

To save a file on Windows just hold down the "ctrl" key and press the "s" key once.

To save a file on a Mac just hold down the "cmd" key and press the "s" key once.

To run a file on Windows press the "F5" key at the top of the keyboard.

On a Mac you can press "F5" as well, but you may need to hold down the "Fn" key at the same time.

5. Now let's try something fancy! Add in some more lines, so your code looks like this:

```
from turtle import *
shape("turtle")
for move in range(6):
    fd(50)
    lt(360/6)
```

> **Loop** Instructions that are followed more than once. It's easier to write a loop than write out your code lots of times. You can use a "for" loop to repeat some code a certain number of times or a "while" loop to keep repeating the code until something happens, such as a variable changing to a certain number.

6. Save your code and run it.

7. Do you see a hexagon being drawn? If not, check your code and try again.

8. You've just made your first loop in Python. The word "for" starts the loop. The phrase "in range (6)" makes the loop repeat 6 times.

A note on colons and spaces

The line of code that starts a loop must always end with a colon ":"

All of the lines underneath it will start with four spaces. IDLE puts these in for you, but if you delete them you can put them back in.

When you have finished writing the loop, remember to stop using four spaces at the start of the next line.

If your computer adds the four lines automatically, press "backspace" to get rid of them.

9. Let's try a different shape. Change your code so that it looks like this:

```
from turtle import *
shape("turtle")
for move in range(5):
    fd(50)
    lt(360/5)
```

10. Can you see how the numbers in the code change the number of sides of the shape? An octagon has 8 sides. Try changing the numbers in your code to make an octagon.

Fun with "for" loops

There are lots of things we can do with loops. Why not try this:

1. Make a new file and call it "star.py" (click on "File" and "New File").

2. Now add in this code. It uses a "**for** **loop**", but this time the distance to move forward is stored as the variable "size."

```python
from turtle import *
shape("turtle")
begin_fill()
size = 100
for move in range(9):
    fd(size)
    rt(160)
```

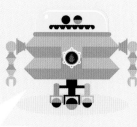

"For" loop Code that repeats instructions a certain number of times

3. This code makes the turtle move forward by 100 and then turn by 160 degrees, and it does this 9 times.

4. Save and run your code to see what it looks like. What happens when you change the value of "size"? Play around with your code and see what you can make.

5. Let's see if we can make it look more interesting with some different colors. Change your code so it looks like this:

```python
from turtle import *
shape("turtle")
color("green","purple")
begin_fill()
size = 100
for move in range(9):
    fd(size)
    rt(160)
end_fill()
```

6. The "color("green","purple")" line makes the turtle draw green lines with a purple fill.

7. The "begin fill()" and "end fill()" commands make the turtle fill in color between the lines.

8. Play around with changing the colors, size, turn, and number of repeats. Can you make more interesting shapes?

9. Can you make your own loop that creates cool patterns and shapes? You can put as many lines of code into a loop as you want; just make sure that each line starts with four spaces. Try this one to start with:

```
from turtle import *
shape("turtle")
color("red","orange")
begin_fill()
for move in range(20):
    fd(120)
    bk(60)
    pu()
    rt(6)
    bk(50)
    pd()
    lt(24)
end_fill()
```

Fun with functions

Functions are a great way of reusing the same code over and over again. They are like the custom blocks you used in Scratch.

1. Create a new file and call it "fun.py."

2. We can start with a simple function to create a square:

```
from turtle import *
shape("turtle")

def square():
    for side in range(4):
        fd(100)
        rt(90)
```

Call Tell a program to follow the instructions in a function

Notice that, like a loop, the function needs a ":" and then four spaces in front of each of the lines inside it.

3. If you run your code now, nothing will happen because we need to call the function—we need to tell the computer to use the function code.

4. This is easy to do! We normally call a function by typing its name followed by (). Change the code so it looks like this:

```
from turtle import *
shape("turtle")

def square():
    for side in range(4):
        fd(100)
        rt(90)

square()
```

5. Run this code to see your square. If it doesn't work, carefully check your code—remember, even the best coders break their code as they learn!

6. Now we have a function to draw a square. We can call the function from inside a loop. Add a few lines to your code so it looks like this:

48

```
from turtle import *
shape("turtle")

def square():
    for side in range(4):
        fd(100)
        rt(90)

for times in range(5):
    square()
    rt(72)
```

7. See if you can make it look a little prettier. Try this to start off with, and then see where your imagination takes you:

```
from turtle import *
shape("turtle")

def square():
    for side in range(4):
        fd(100)
        rt(90)

color("purple","green")
begin_fill()

for times in range(5):
    square()
    rt(72)

end_fill()
```

Turtle illusions

This time we're going to make an optical illusion using our turtle. Once you're done, see if you can impress your friends with it.

1. Create a new file and save it as "illusion.py."

2. We can start with a few extra commands to set up our program. Try this:

```
from turtle import *
speed(10)
bgcolor("black")
width(10)
```

This sets our turtle to a faster speed, so the drawing doesn't take too long. It also sets the background color to black and the pen width to 10.

3. The first thing we want to do is draw a thick and very long line. Can you change your code so that it looks like this?

```
from turtle import *
speed(10)
bgcolor("black")
width(10)

def line():
    color("gray")
    fd(800)
    bk(2000)
    fd(1200)
```

4. Nothing will happen when you run the file because we haven't called "line()." If you want to test out the code, try typing "line()" into the shell.

5. Now we want to use our line function to draw lots of lines. Change your code so it looks like this (see next page):

```
from turtle import *

speed(10)
bgcolor("black")
width(10)

def line():
    color("gray")
    fd(800)
    bk(2000)
    fd(1200)

def lines():
    pu()
    goto(-300,300)
    pd()
    for times in range(7):
        line()
        pu()
        rt(90)
        fd(100)
        lt(90)
        pd()
```

```
def line():
    color("gray")
    fd(800)
    bk(2000)
    fd(1200)

def lines():
    pu()
    goto(-300,300)
    pd()
    for times in range(7):
        line()
        pu()
        rt(90)
        fd(100)
        lt(90)
        pd()

def grid():
    lines()
    lt(90)
    lines()
```

6. Here we move the turtle to the corner of the screen, and then tell it to draw our lines 7 times. After each line is drawn, the turtle moves down a little. Again, if you want to see the lines being drawn, save and run your file, then type "lines()" into the shell.

7. Now we're going to use our lines function to draw a grid. Add a new function so that your code looks like this:

```
from turtle import *

speed(10)
bgcolor("black")
width(10)
```

8. Save and run your code, then type "grid()" into the shell to make sure your grid is being drawn.

9. Now we're going to create a function to put dots in the grid. This will help create the visual illusion itself. Add a function to your code so that it is the same as the one below:

```
from turtle import *

speed(10)
bgcolor("black")
width(10)
```

```
def line():
    color("gray")
    fd(800)
    bk(2000)
    fd(1200)

def lines():
    pu()
    goto(-300,300)
    pd()
    for times in range(7):
        line()
        pu()
        rt(90)
        fd(100)
        lt(90)
        pd()

def grid():
    lines()
    lt(90)
    lines()

def dots():
    color("white")
    pu()
    goto(-300,300)
    setheading(0)
    for i in range(7):
        for i in range(7):
            dot(20)
            fd(100)
        rt(90)
        fd(100)
        lt(90)
        bk(700)

grid()
dots()
```

This uses a "for" loop inside another "for" loop, so check that you have the correct number of spaces before each line. On the next line, "dot(20)" adds a size-20 dot onto the screen. The last two lines call our functions.

10. Run your code and see what happens. What color do the circles look like to you? Ask someone else to have a look at your optical illusion and see what they think!

Can you take a challenge?

- What happens to your optical illusion if you change the size of the dots? What happens if you change the colors of the lines?

- Look on the Internet for images of other optical illusions. Can you try and create one of your own? How about something like this?

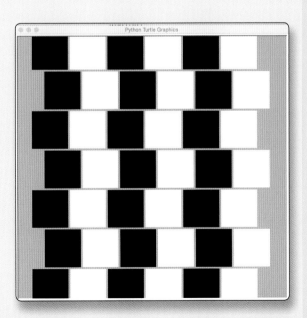

Fun with strings

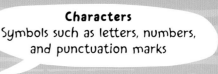

Characters
Symbols such as letters, numbers, and punctuation marks

What are strings?

In programming, the word string is short for "a string of characters." Characters are all the letters and symbols you can see on your keyboard (a–z, 0–9) plus others that you don't see, like 🖤 or 😊. A string is just one or more characters put together. In Python, strings are always surrounded with double or single quotation marks. You can use either, but keep them the same on each line of code, like this:

"Hello World!"

'I love Python'

Input and output

String
Sequence of characters

We can use Python to output strings. Let's try making some of our own.

1. Open IDLE and create a new file.

2. Save your file as "pippa.py."

3. Now type this into your new file:

   ```python
   print("My name is Pippa the Python")
   ```

4. Save and run your file, and the words should be printed in the shell.

5. We can also get strings from the user, and save them as a variable. Try this:

   ```python
   print("My name is Pippa the Python")
   name = input("What is your name?")
   print("Nice to meet you," name)
   ```

   User
   Person using a computer or program

6. When you save and run the file, the first line will be output to the shell. Then in the shell you can type your name, and Pippa should reply to you.

7. What if we want Pippa to say different things depending on who she is talking to? We can use "if" statements to do this. We use a double equal sign (==) to see if "name" is equal to "Poly." In Python, a single equal sign is used to set a variable, and a double equal sign is used to test if two things are the same.

   ```python
   print("My name is Pippa the Python")
   name = input("What is your name?")
   if name == "Poly":
       print("You are an awesome coder,", name)
   else:
       print("Yuck,", name, "is a horrible name.")
   ```

8. You can change the name "Poly" to your own name, and then save and run your code.

9. Try typing in your own name and then running it again. Get a friend or someone in your family to type in their name.

Random replies

1. Let's make our code a little more interesting!

   Add in a line at the top of your program, so it looks like this:

   ```
   from random import *
   print("My name is Pippa the Python")
   name = input("What is your name?")
   if name == "Poly":
       print("You are an awesome coder", name)
   else:
       print("Hmm,", name, "that is not the name I expected.")
   ```

2. Now we can add some nice things for Pippa to say. We'll put the things to say in a list, which is surrounded by "[ ]." Then we use the "choice( )" command to pick a random thing from the list.

   ```
   from random import *

   praise = choice(["You are cool", "You are amazing", "You sound lovely"])

   print("My name is Pippa the Python")

   name = input("What is your name?")
   if name == "Poly":
       print("You are an awesome coder,", name)
   else:
       print("Hmm,", name, "that is not the name I expected.")
   ```

3. Then we can use the nice things in Pippa's reply.

   ```
   from random import *

   praise = choice(["You are cool", "You are amazing", "You sound lovely"])
   print("My name is Pippa the Python")
   name = input("What is your name?")
   if name == "Poly":
       print(praise,name)
   else:
       print("Hmm,", name, " that is not the name I expected.")
   ```

4. Save and run your code to make sure it is all working.

5. Add some more nice things for Pippa to say into the list.

6. We can make Pippa reject people as well. Change your code so it looks like this:

```
from random import *

praise = choice(["You are cool",
"You are amazing", "You sound lovely"])
denied = choice(["Access denied", "You're not allowed here",
"Abort, abort"])
print("My name is Pippa the Python")
name = input("What is your name?")
if name == "Poly":
    print(praise, name)
else:
    print(denied, name)
```

7. Save and run your code and then test it on yourself, your friends, and your family.

8. Add more random phrases to the list, to make it more interesting.

Rock, paper, scissors

We can use what we have learned so far to make a game of rock, paper, scissors!

1. Create a new file and save it as "game.py."

2. We are going to need the random module again:

```
from random import *
items = ["ROCK", "PAPER", "SCISSORS"]
print("Welcome to rock, paper, scissors")
```

3. Save and run your game, to make sure it works so far.

4. Now let's find out if the player wants to choose rock, paper, or scissors.
```
items = ["ROCK", "PAPER", "SCISSORS"]
print("Welcome to rock, paper, scissors")
player = input("Choose rock, paper, or scissors")
print("You chose",player)
```

5. Save and run your code. In the shell you can type your choice of rock, paper, or scissors.

6. A computer can't tell that the word "ROCK" is the same as "rock," so we need to change the input so

   that it is all in capital letters. We can use the ".upper()" command to do this:

```
from random import *

items = ["ROCK", "PAPER", "SCISSORS")
print("Welcome to rock, paper, scissors")
player = input("Choose rock, paper, or scissors").upper()
print("You chose",player)
```

7. Save and run your code again. If you type in "rock," it should convert it to "ROCK."

8. But what if the player types something other than rock, paper, or scissors? We'll have to change our code so that it handles this!

```
from random import *

items = ["ROCK", "PAPER", "SCISSORS"]
print("Welcome to rock, paper, scissors")
player = ''
while player not in items:
    player = input("Choose rock, paper, or scissors").upper()
print("You chose",player)
```

9. Here we are using a new loop called a "while" loop. The line inside the "while" loop will keep running until the player chooses something from the list. Save and run your code and then test it with the word "rock" and then again with the misspelled word "roc" to make sure it asks you to choose again.

10. Now the computer needs to make a "choice()." This code picks a random item from the list:

```
from random import *

items = ["ROCK", "PAPER", "SCISSORS"]
print("Welcome to rock, paper, scissors")
player = ''
while player not in items:
    player = input("Choose rock, paper or scissors").upper()
print("You chose",player)
computer = choice(items)
print("I choose",computer)
```

Dictionary
A way of organizing data so that keys and values are linked together

11. Let's work out who has won the game! To start with, we need to write down the rules. We will use a dictionary for this. A dictionary is like a list, but it can store keys and values. You could use a dictionary to store people's ages, for instance {"Marc":10, "Poly":7, "Lisa":9} or to store words that rhyme {"cat":"bat","fall":"tall","red":"bed"}. The dictionary will tell us what beats what in

this game. A dictionary is surrounded by { }.

```
from random import *

items = ["ROCK","PAPER","SCISSORS"]
print("Welcome to rock, paper, scissors")
player = ''
while player not in items:
    player = input("Choose rock, paper, or scissors").upper()
print("You chose",player)
computer = choice(items)
print("I choose",computer)

rules = {"ROCK":"SCISSORS","PAPER":"ROCK","SCISSORS":"PAPER"}
```

The rule dictionary has pairings of words inside it. "ROCK":"SCISSORS" tells us that "ROCK" beats "SCISSORS." "PAPER":"ROCK" means that "PAPER" beats "ROCK."

12. To finish, we can use "if" statements to see who has won the game. When multiple "if" statements determine an outcome, "elif" is a contraction for "else if." If the player and computer choices are the same (player == computer), then it's a draw. Otherwise, the program can use the dictionary to see who has won:

```
from random import *

items = ["ROCK","PAPER","SCISSORS"]
print("Welcome to rock, paper, scissors")
player = ''
while player not in items:
    player = input("Choose rock, paper, or scissors").upper()
print("You chose",player)
computer = choice(items)
print("I choose",computer)
rules = {"ROCK":"SCISSORS","PAPER":"ROCK","SCISSORS":"PAPER"}

if player == computer:
    print("We drew")
elif rules[player] == computer:
    print("You won")
else:
    print("I won")
```

13. Save and run the game. Well done! You have made your first Python computer game. You have made amazing progress.

Can you take a challenge?

- Can you use a variable to keep track of the player's score and a "while" loop to keep the game running until the player has scored five points?

- How about adding in more choices and rules? Look up the rules for "Rock, Paper, Scissors, Lizard, Spock" on the Internet.

Programming in the real world

What are hackers?

You've probably heard the word "hackers" before, but very few people understand what it really means. People think of hackers as nasty programmers who use their coding skills to break the law and steal people's information, or sometimes even their money. This is because we often see stories in the newspapers or on television about criminals who have hacked into people's computers.

Hackers Experts at using a computer

Many programmers proudly call themselves hackers. They don't do anything illegal with computers; they just write code that does clever or unusual things.

Other programmers are very interested in writing code to break into computers or to take advantage of mistakes in other people's programs so that they can take control of a computer.

Hackers can fall into two different groups:

Black hat hackers

Black hat hackers use their skills to break the law. They sometimes write programs that take control of other people's computers or steal information from computers. Sometimes they'll write programs called **malware** that can stop your computer from working or make it behave in strange ways, like opening websites that you didn't ask to be opened.

Black hat hackers Hackers who use their skills to commit crimes

Malware Computer programs that do bad things to computers

There are two main ways that a black hat hacker can access other people's computers. Sometimes people have simple passwords that are easy to guess, or people can be tricked into telling the black hat what their password is. Another way of accessing somebody else's computer is to use what is known as a **zero-day exploit**. A zero-day exploit is a mistake that a programmer has made in their code, and because they didn't know about the mistake, they've had zero days to fix it. Until the code is fixed, a zero-day exploit can be used by a hacker to cause havoc.

Zero-day exploit Mistake in some software that the creator doesn't know about and has had zero days to fix

White hat hackers

White hat hackers have the same skills as black hat hackers, but they don't break the law. Instead, when white hat hackers find zero-day exploits, they tell the programmers who made the software, so that the programmers can fix the mistakes in their code. This prevents black hat hackers from using the zero-day exploit in the future. Most companies will pay white hat hackers lots of money to find zero-day exploits.

There are even competitions for white hat hackers, with thousands of dollars in prize money for the ones who find the most zero-day exploits. White hat hackers are like the superheroes of the hacking world!

Indie and AAA game programmers

Many people first start learning to code because they want to make computer games. Maybe that's why you are reading this book right now! If you become a game developer, you might want to make either indie games or AAA games.

Indie games

Indie game developers work on their own, or with a few friends, to create their games. They do all the work themselves, from writing the code to creating the graphics and thinking up the story. Indie developers don't work for any single company, so they are free to make whatever games they like, for consoles, tablets, phones, or PCs.

Some indie games become extremely popular and can make the developers a lot of money. Sometimes the developers will give away their games for free because they care more about the art of making games than making money. Indie developers might also sell just a few games to their fans. Probably the most successful and famous indie game of all time is Minecraft.

AAA games

AAA games are made by large companies. These are the games that you see advertized on TV and that can sell millions of copies. AAA games are made by huge teams of people. There are programmers to write the code, artists to make the 3D characters and scenery, writers to create the stories, musicians to compose the music, designers to design the levels, and then other huge teams in charge of advertizing and selling the game.

Programmers who work for AAA game companies will often be in charge of one very small element of a game. They might be experts in creating realistic water, or creating the rules that decide how the non-player characters act, or even something as specific as how to make flags flutter in the wind.

What is Free and Open Source Software?

If you become a programmer, you will be able to work on **Free and Open Source Software (FOSS)**. These are programs written by coders either on their own or with the help of lots of other coders. Free and Open Source Software is free for people to use, copy, and share. Best of all, you are also allowed to look through the code and make improvements to it.

FOSS is really important. Most of the websites you visit on the Internet are sitting on servers that run on GNU/Linux.

Free and Open Source Software (FOSS) Computer programs that you are allowed to look at, change, use, and share

This is a FOSS group of operating systems and it is improved every day by thousands of programmers from all over the world. Do you or somebody in your family own an Android cell phone? That phone runs lots of FOSS. Do you use Firefox as your web browser? This is also based on FOSS.

Lots of people and companies help to make FOSS. Some people do it for fun, others do it because they want to help the programming community, and others do it as their job.

A secret key

Encryption is a way of changing information so that nobody else can read it unless they have the secret key.

Imagine you wanted to send a friend the message:

"Meet me at the park at three"

but you didn't want anyone else to be able to read it. You could use a simple method of encryption to

Encryption Disguising data so that it is impossible to read without knowing how it has been disguised

disguise your message. For instance, you could use a key of 5 and then move each letter of your message forward five letters in the alphabet, as shown here:

abcdefghijklmnopqrstuvwxyz

fghijklmnopqrstuvwxyzabcde

So:

"Meet me at the park at three"

would become:

"Rjjy rj fy ymj ufwp fy ymwjj"

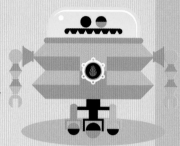

If your friend knows the key is 5, then they could easily **decrypt** your message to read its real meaning!

Encryption used today is much more complicated than this method, which was originally used by Julius Caesar, the Roman Emperor, to send messages to his generals. This method, called the **Caesar cipher,** would be really easy to decrypt just by trying all 26 possible keys and seeing which key made sense of the message.

Decrypt Make encrypted data readable

Programmers now create methods of encrypting information that are so complicated, it is impossible to crack them without having the key. This is really important, especially when you are using the Internet. When you send messages back and forth on the Internet, it is really easy for another person (maybe a black hat) to see your message. This could mean that someone could see what you were doing when you were typing in your password, doing some shopping, or using your bank. To stop other people being able to read the messages your computer sends out over the Internet, the information is usually encrypted.

You'll know if you are using encryption on the Internet because the bar at the top of your web browser will say https:// instead of just http://. You might also see a little padlock symbol like this, which tells you that you are using encryption: 🔒 https: .

Web development

Web developers make web pages that work in a web browser. Many web developers build web pages in a language called JavaScript. You can also build some basic web pages by coding in a language called HTML. HTML stands for Hypertext Markup Language. It's not a programming language because you can't actually write programs with it. Instead your web browser turns HTML into normal words and pictures that you can understand.

To make a web page, you are going to need to use a text editor. If you are using Windows then you could use Notepad. On a Mac, you could use TextEdit. There are other text editors that are even better, though, so you might want to search for Sublime Text or Atom and download either of those instead. Remember to always ask an adult before downloading new programs onto your computer; this helps to keep your computer healthy!

1. Open up your text editor, make a new folder to save your web pages in, and then try writing the following few lines:

```
<html>
<body>
<h1>This is my first web page</h1>
<p>This is a page all about me</p>
</body>
</html>
```

2. Save your file as "index.html"—don't forget the .html ending! Look in the folder you have made and double-click on your file to open it in a web browser. It should look something like this:

index.html - Google Chrome
index.html
file:///home/coding2learn/Dropbox/Introduction%20to%20co

This is my first web page

This is a page all about me

3. There are lots of tags that you can try out. Open your text editor again. This time try adding these lines between your "<body>" and "<body>" tags.

```
<em>I'm learning how to code.</em>
<a href="https://www.codecademy.com/">
And here is a good site to learn
from.</a>
```

4. Save your web page and then take another look at it in your browser.

If you want to learn more about coding HTML, there are lots of online resources to help you out.

Find out more

Snap!

If you liked Scratch, then you'll love Snap! It is another programming language that is very similar to Scratch. You can have a look at Snap! by going to http://snap.berkeley.edu/ in a web browser. Snap! is a little more complicated than Scratch, but it is also more powerful—you can do more things with it.

Snap! Programming language similar to Scratch

Touch Develop

If you want to write code on a tablet or phone and build apps that will run on mobile devices, then you should have a look at Touch Develop. You can play with Touch Develop by creating an account at https://www.touchdevelop.com/app/. Touch Develop has two modes—a Scratch-like mode that lets you drag and drop blocks, and a mode that lets you write scripts like you did in Python.

Touch Develop Programming language similar to Scratch that is designed to be used on smartphones and tablets

Making games with Pygame Zero

If you want to make computer games, then you should have a look at Pygame Zero. You can get instructions for installing Pygame Zero and some tutorials by going to http://pygame-zero.readthedocs.org/. Start off by asking an adult to help you install it on your computer. With Pygame Zero you can make games that use graphics and images and respond to key presses and mouse clicks.

The Raspberry Pi

This isn't a dessert—the Raspberry Pi is actually a tiny computer that can help you learn to code. There are hundreds of resources online to teach you how to code on the Raspberry Pi, and https://www.raspberrypi.org is a good place to start. The Raspberry Pi has input and output pins, which allow you to connect all types of devices and electronic components. This means you can write code to do anything from turning on a few lights to controlling a robot on the Internet.

Raspberry Pi Cheap, credit-card-size computer, designed to help people learn how to program

Codecademy

Codecademy at https://www.codecademy.com is a website that can help you learn to code. There are lots of things to learn about on this website: you can learn more HTML and JavaScript if you want to learn about web development. You could also improve your Python skills or learn a new programming language like Ruby.

Codecademy Website that teaches you to code in many different programming languages

Pygame Zero Library that makes writing games in Python easier

Glossary

Algorithm Set of instructions to perform a task

Black hat hackers Hackers who use their skills to commit crimes

Block Palette Area in the Scratch GUI that contains the blocks that can be used in a script

Caesar cipher Way of encrypting words by replacing the letters with other letters

Call Tell a program to follow the instructions in a function

Characters Symbols such as letters, numbers, and punctuation marks

Clones Copies of a sprite and all its scripts

Code Instructions written in a programming language that a computer can follow

Codecademy Website that teaches you to code in many different programming languages

Coding Writing code for a computer

Compiling Converting a program into a language that a computer can run

Custom block Scratch block that does a specific task

Debugging Testing code to find and fix mistakes

Decrypt Make encrypted data readable

Dictionary Way of organizing data so that keys and values are linked together

Encryption Disguising data so that it is impossible to read without knowing the secret key (how it has been disguised)

"For" loop Code that repeats instructions a certain number of times

Fractal Never-ending and repeating pattern

Free and Open Source Software (FOSS) Software that you are allowed to look at, change, use, and share

GNU/Linux Free and Open Source operating system used on many computers around the world

Graphical User Interface (GUI) Screen that lets you click buttons or choose items from a menu, usually using your mouse, trackpad, or touch screen

Hackers Experts at using a computer

Input Data that is received by a computer program

Interpreting When a program is run by a computer, one line at a time

Loop Instructions that are followed more than once

Malware Computer programs that do bad things to computers

Module Code written by other people that you can use in your own programs

Operating system Software that manages a computer, such as Windows, OS X, and GNU/Linux

Passphrase Group of words that is easy to remember but hard for someone else to guess

Program Design and write code

Programmer Person who designs and writes code

Programs Collections of instructions that a computer follows to perform a task

Pygame Zero Library that makes writing games in Python easier

Python Programming language based on typing text, designed to be simple to learn and use

Raspberry Pi Cheap, credit-card-size computer, designed to help people learn how to program

Scratch Programming language created for children that uses blocks of code that can be connected together to make programs

Script Small section of code, which can be as short as a few lines or as long as hundreds of lines; in Scratch, a script is a collection of blocks that you have joined together

Script Area Area in the Scratch GUI where blocks can be assembled into scripts

Shell Program that follows written instructions

Snap! Programming language similar to Scratch

Software A computer program or collection of computer programs

Sprites Images used in computer games

Sprites Pane Area in the Scratch GUI where available sprites can be seen

Stage Area in the Scratch GUI where you can see your project running

String Sequence of characters

Syntax The rules of a programming language

Syntax error Mistake in a computer program caused by not following the rules of the programming language

Touch Develop Programming language similar to Scratch that is designed to be used on smartphones and tablets

User Person using a computer or program

Variable Symbol or name that represents a value

"While" loop Code that will keep repeating until something happens, such as a variable changing to a certain number

White hat hackers Hackers who use their skills to protect people

Zero-day exploit Mistake in some software that the creator doesn't know about and has had zero days to fix

Index